Porcupines

Sara Antill

WINDMILL BOOKS

New York

Published in 2011 by Windmill Books, LLC
303 Park Avenue South, Suite # 1280, New York, NY 10010-3657

First Edition

CREDITS:
Author: Sara Antill
Edited by: Jennifer Way
Designed by: Brian Garvey

Photo Credits: Cover, pp. 7 (main, inset), 8-9, 9 (inset), 11 (bottom), 12-13 (main), 17 (top, bottom), 19 (top, bottom), p. 22 (bottom) Shutterstock.com; p. 4 © www.iStockphoto.com/Jonathan Heger, p. 5 © www.iStockphoto.com/Sara Robinson; p. 6 Steve Winter/Getty Images; pp. 10, 22 (top) Tim Jackson/Getty Images; p. 11 (top) David Cavagnaro/Getty Images; p. 12 (inset) © www.iStockphoto.com/Jan Gottwald; p. 13 (inset) Frank Schneidermeyer/Getty Images; p. 14 © Philippe Henry/age fotostock; p. 15 © www.iStockphoto.com/Alain Turgeon; p. 16 © S.J. Krasemann/Peter Arnold Inc.; pp. 18-19 © www.iStockphoto.com/Megan Lorenz; pp. 20-21 © Huetter, C/age fotostock.

Library of Congress Cataloging-in-Publication Data

Antill, Sara.
Porcupines / by Sara Antill. — 1st ed.
      p. cm. — (Unusual animals)
Includes index.
ISBN 978-1-60754-995-6 (library binding) — ISBN 978-1-61533-005-8 (pbk.) —
ISBN 978-1-61533-006-5 (6-pack)
1. Porcupines I. Title.
QL737.R652A68 2011
599.35'97—dc22
                              2010004894

Manufactured in the United States of America

For more great fiction and nonfiction, go to windmillbooks.com.

CPSIA Compliance Information: Batch #B W2011WM: For Further Information contact Windmill Books, New York, New York at 1-866-478-0556

Table of Contents

Making a Point!

Porcupines are strange-looking animals. Their bodies are covered with sharp, needle-like spines called **quills**.

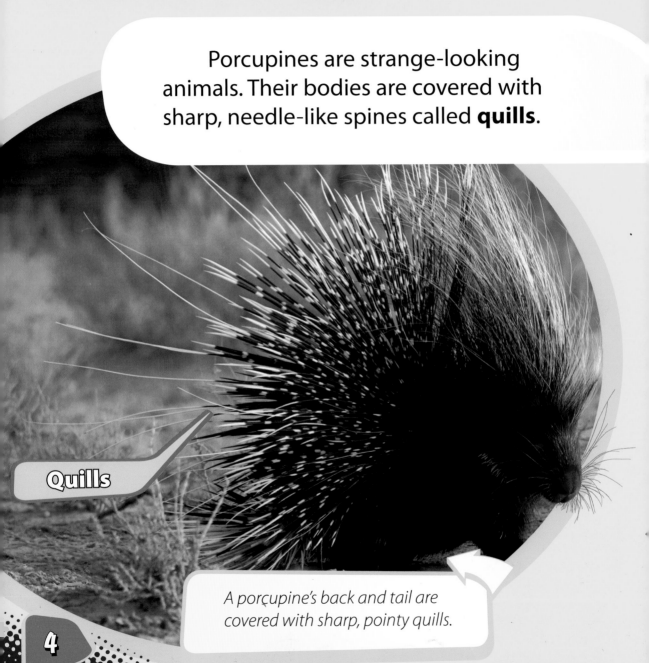

Quills

A porcupine's back and tail are covered with sharp, pointy quills.

The porcupine actually got its name because of its quills. "Porcupine" means "spined pig." However, porcupines aren't related to pigs at all!

The porcupine is a **rodent**. Rodents are animals, such as mice and squirrels, that use their four long front teeth to gnaw on wood and plants.

This porcupine is crawling across a boy's shoulder.

Porcupines are small animals. Their bodies are about 25 to 36 inches (60–90 cm) long. Their tails are about 8 to 10 inches (20–25 cm) long. A full-grown porcupine can weigh 12 to 35 pounds (5–16 kg).

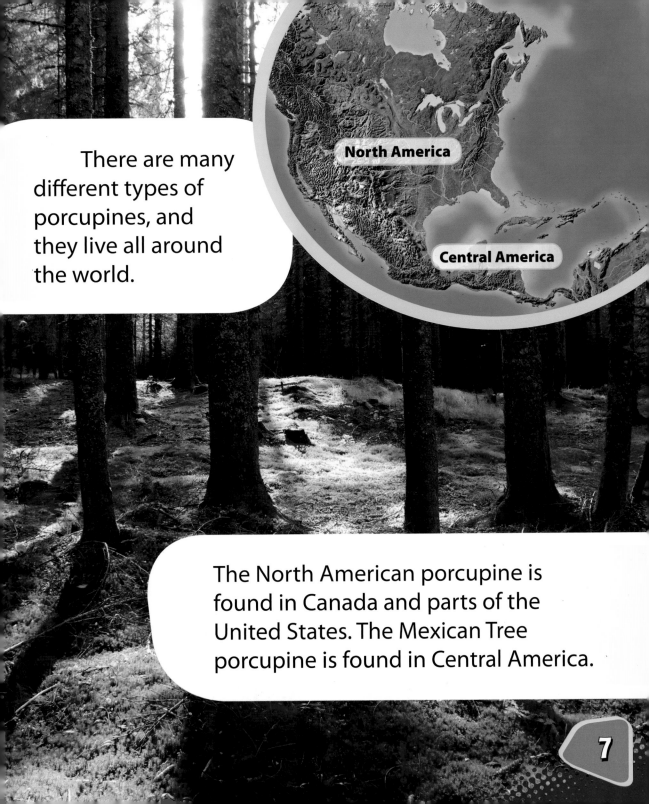

There are many different types of porcupines, and they live all around the world.

North America

Central America

The North American porcupine is found in Canada and parts of the United States. The Mexican Tree porcupine is found in Central America.

The first things you may notice about a porcupine are its sharp quills. Quills are thick, hollow hairs with prickly, pointy tips. When a porcupine quill gets stuck in another animal's skin, small **barbs** on the end make it hard to pull out.

Here is a close-up view of a porcupine's quills.

A porcupine has about 30,000 quills covering its body! When one of the quills falls out, another one grows to replace it.

These porcupines have raised their quills to scare away a lion.

A porcupine uses its quills to protect itself from danger. When a **predator** comes too close, the porcupine will turn its back and raise its quills. It will even shake its tail to let the other animal know it isn't fooling around!

The porcupine can't shoot its quills, but they do come loose very easily.

This dog tried to attack a porcupine and got a face full of quills!

If a quill gets stuck in an animal's skin, it will dig deeper and deeper into the animal's body. If this happens, the animal can die.

Living the High Life

Porcupines live in **deciduous** forests. These are forests made up of trees that lose their leaves once a year.

Porcupines make their dens in caves, logs, and hollow trees.

These porcupines are sleeping in their den.

This porcupine is out in the snow looking for food.

They stay active during the winter, but they will stay inside their dens when the weather gets bad.

Porcupines are very good climbers. They spend most of their time in trees.

Some porcupines in South America, such as the Brazilian porcupine, use their tails to grip branches. This helps them keep their balance when they are climbing.

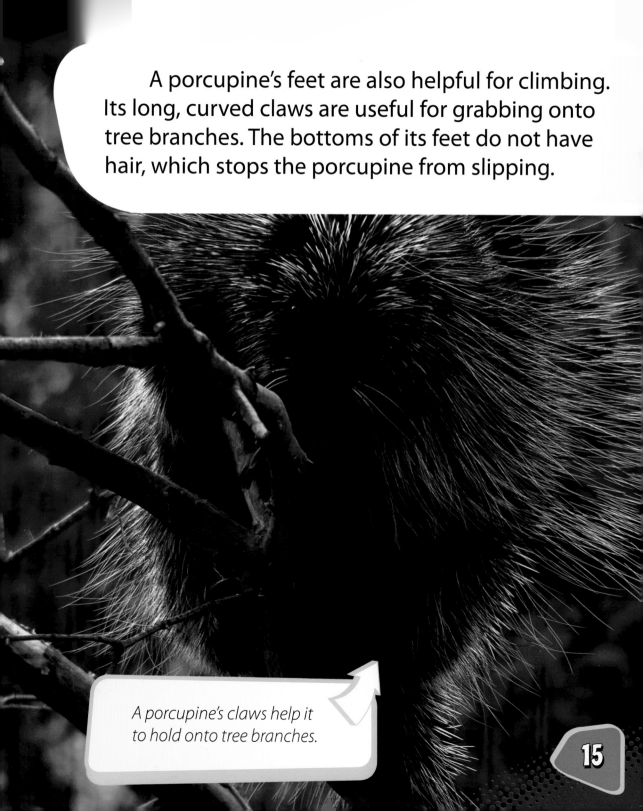

A porcupine's feet are also helpful for climbing. Its long, curved claws are useful for grabbing onto tree branches. The bottoms of its feet do not have hair, which stops the porcupine from slipping.

A porcupine's claws help it to hold onto tree branches.

Porcupines have strong teeth that they use to chew on wood and other plant matter.

Like many rodents, porcupines are **herbivorous**. They use their strong teeth to chew on bark, stems, and twigs. They also eat fruit, leaves, and roots.

Most of the food that porcupines eat does not have a lot of salt. To make up for this, porcupines will sometimes lick animal bones or eat the salt that is put on roads to melt ice.

They will even chew on tool handles that people have touched because the sweat from our hands has salt in it!

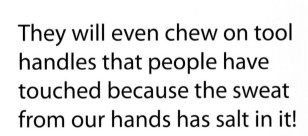

A porcupine might want to munch on this man's ax after he's done using it!

Cycle of Life

Porcupines have many natural predators. Wolves, coyotes, mountain lions, and great horned owls will all take their chances against the porcupine's dangerous quills.

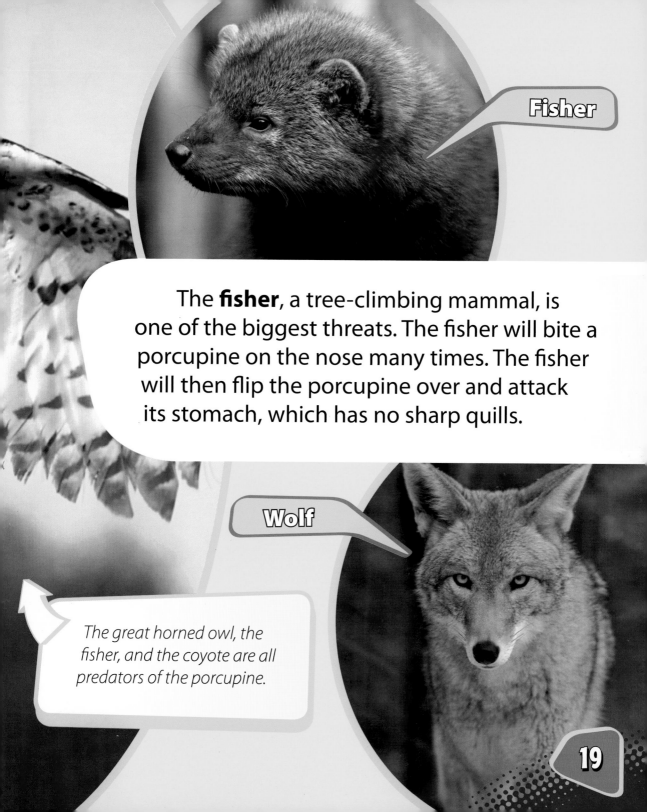

Fisher

The **fisher**, a tree-climbing mammal, is one of the biggest threats. The fisher will bite a porcupine on the nose many times. The fisher will then flip the porcupine over and attack its stomach, which has no sharp quills.

Wolf

The great horned owl, the fisher, and the coyote are all predators of the porcupine.

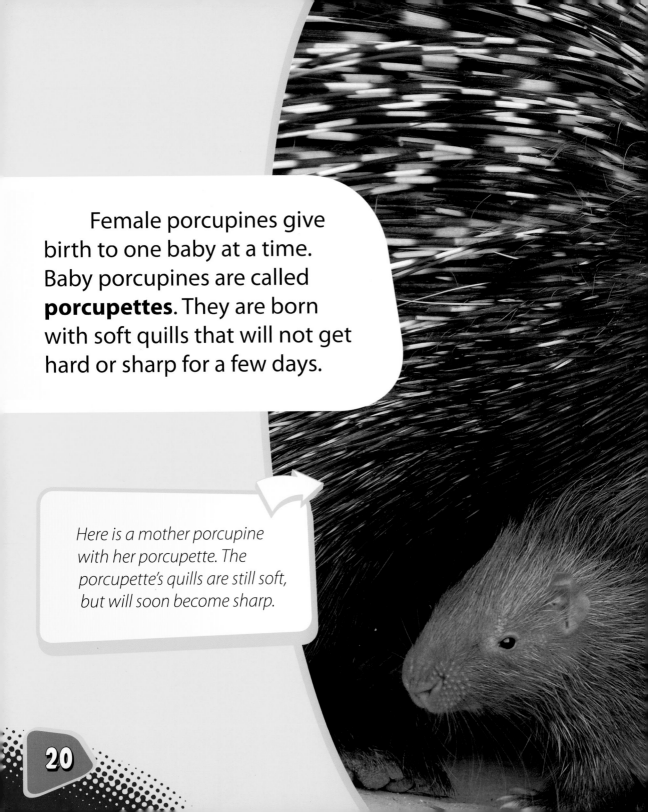

Female porcupines give birth to one baby at a time. Baby porcupines are called **porcupettes**. They are born with soft quills that will not get hard or sharp for a few days.

Here is a mother porcupine with her porcupette. The porcupette's quills are still soft, but will soon become sharp.

After just 10 days, a porcupette is ready to eat solid food and climb trees with its mother. It will stay with her until it is about 2 months old. Once the young porcupine has learned to survive, it will go out into the forest to live on its own.

Inside Story

The crested porcupine in Africa has the longest quills. They can be almost 12 inches (30 cm) long!

Porcupines move slowly on land, but they are very good swimmers. Their hollow quills help them float.

Porcupines can live for up to 20 years.

Porcupines make a lot of noise. They moan, grunt, growl, wail, whine, and chatter their teeth!

Glossary

BARB (BARB) A sharp point that sticks out in the opposite direction of the main point, like an arrow or fishhook, and makes the object hard to remove.

DECIDUOUS (dih-SID-ju-us) A tree or plant that loses its leaves every year.

FISHER (FIH-shur) A small animal, related to the weasel, that will attack porcupines.

HERBIVOROUS (her-BIH-ver-us) Something that eats plants.

PORCUPETTE (por-kyu-PET) A baby porcupine.

PREDATOR (PREH-da-tur) An animal who hunts another animal for food.

QUILL (KWIL) Thick, hollow hair with a sharp, pointed tip.

RODENT (ROW-dent) A type of mammal that has two long front teeth in each jaw, used for gnawing.

Index

Read More

Nichols, Catherine. *Prickly Porcupines*. New York: Bearport Publishing, 2008.

Tagliaferro, Linda. *Explore the Deciduous Forest*. Mankato, MN: Capstone Press, 2007.

Webster, Christine. *Porcupines*. New York: Weigl Publishing, 2009.

Web Sites

For Web resources related to the subject of this book, go to: www.windmillbooks.com/weblinks and select this book's title.